£1-50

World Link Meditation

Healing Yourself and Others

Mantak Chia

Table of Contents

Introduction:

My wish is for every person to be spiritually independent by connecting directly to the Source, Cosmos, Primordial Force, or Creative Force in our common quest for return to the *Wu Chi* (God). Through this process we can gain inner peace and happiness. Everyone can gain the ability not only to heal themselves, but others too. Naturally, the first step is to be at peace and be happy with ourselves as we work to accomplish our goals. Therefore, I have devised this meditation, which becomes especially profound when its effect is amplified by thousands of others in a ***Circle of Consciousness and Awareness.*** It is the ***International Healing Tao World Link.*** We always start with the Protective Sacred Circle of Fire. It creates a fence of protection allowing only the good energy and good intentions in. Negative energy can't penetrate the circle.

The universe has abundant energy to enhance and multiply our life. All that we need to do is to be connected to the source. It helps to understand the principle of fusing the three minds. Western science now knows there are three minds. The first mind is in the observing mind centered in the brain. The second is called the conscious mind centered in the heart. The third is the mind of awareness centered in the lower abdomen, that is, the abdominal brain. The three minds combine to fuse together in the abdomen, creating one mind. In Chinese this one mind is called ***Yi***. The World Link of Protection Healing Meditation is a spiritual practice that takes around 15 to 30 minutes. When people from all around the world link together at the same time with this meditation, the meditation is greatly empowered. This meditation can be practiced easily even by those who have never worked with the International Healing Tao practices.

Link Time: Thailand 12:00 Noon; New York 12:00 Midnight; Europe 6:00 a.m. in the Morning. Find your Time Zone and it can be one hour before or after these morning and evening times.

Explanation:

The ***Three Minds*** are the ***Upper, Middle & Lower*** or the ***Three Tan Tiens***. Upper Mind is good for planning and figuring out numbers, but with the negative emotions, it stirs up the brain with excess thinking and worrying. It spends and drains out too much energy. We should train this brain while resting to just observe. The key is to lower your Upper Mind and use it in the Lower Mind to do your thinking.

At first, I did not understand this. When my Master taught me to lower and sink my mind down to the lower Tan Tien, I started to understand. Later, I understood this further, when I found that Western technology had discovered that the nerve endings in the stomach and intestines, especially related to emotional responses, are the same as those in the Upper Mind. So by just smiling to the lower Tan Tien you can activate the Lower Mind. By using the awareness, consciousness, and observing minds together in the abdomen you can do all your thinking.

The Upper Mind works practically all the time, stirring up the emotions and using up to 80% of your body energy. Western science has discovered that the lower mind can do a lot of things that the Upper Mind does without using the senses. The difference is it does it with pure awareness without questioning, as the Upper Mind does. If you can use the lower brain more, the Upper Mind can rest and listen (observe) from the abdomen. The Upper Mind, or as the Taoists refer to it, the monkey mind, when activated will suppress consciousness or awareness. Once the Upper Mind rests you can be conscious and aware of things you were never conscious or aware of before. You then can rest, be more aware, and save energy using the lower (second) brain. So your upper brain can rest and build up strength for any daily stress.

The Three Minds

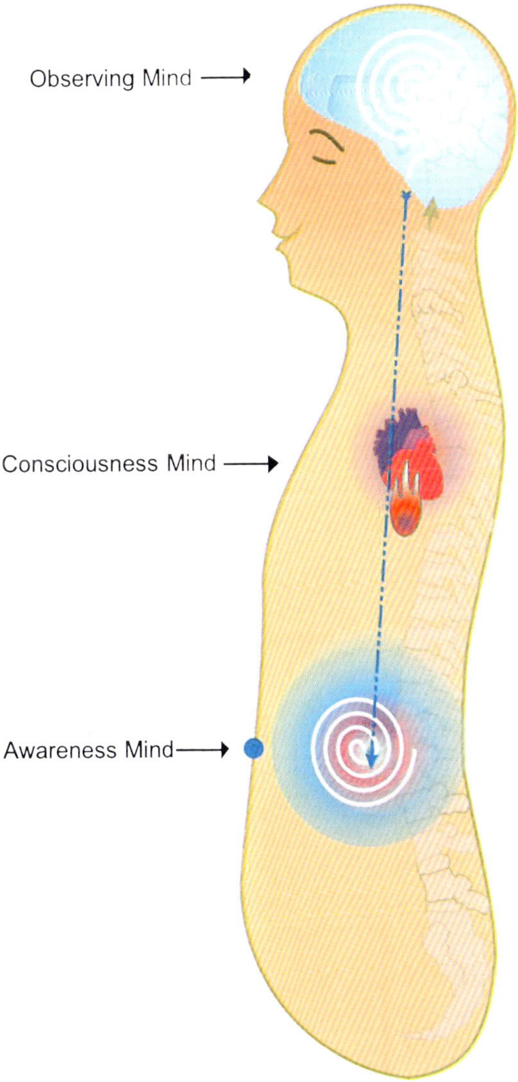

Empty your mind down to the Tan Tien.
Let the awareness and consciousness combine together.

Preparation:

Stand or sit alone or with others in a group meditation. Relax and empty your mind down to the Tan Tien by smiling down to your lower abdomen. Bring your awareness to your abdomen and fill your abdominal brain with Chi.

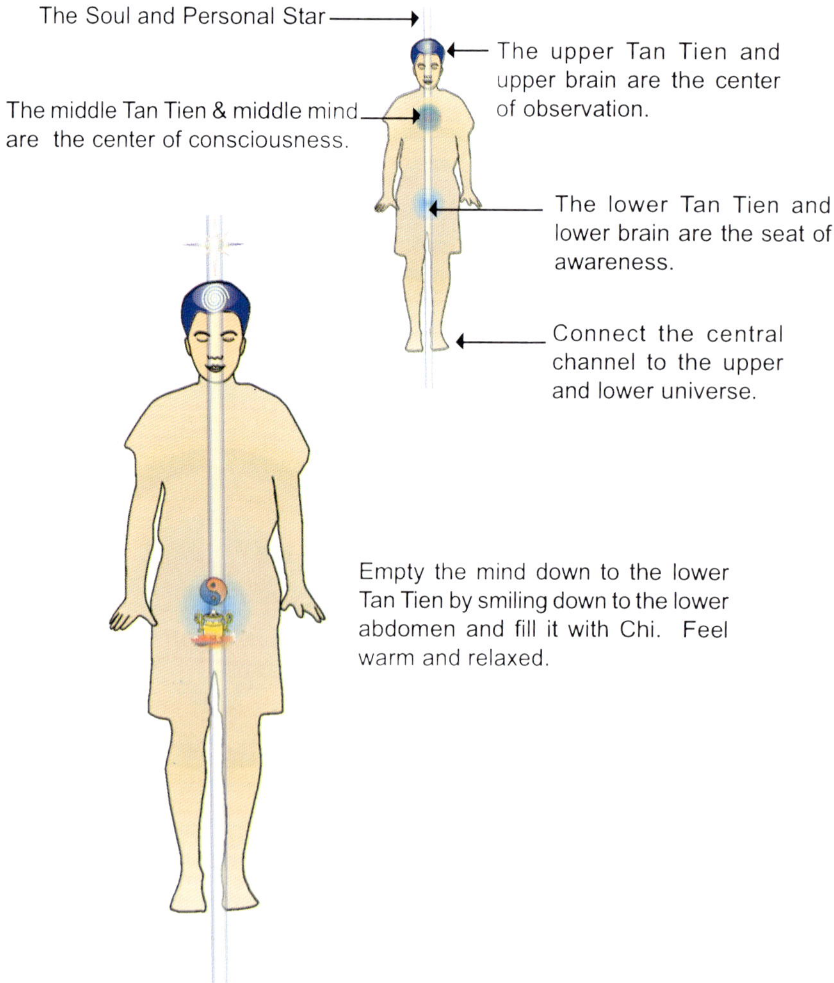

Activate the Consciousness of the Three Fires:

Tan Tien, Kidney and Heart Fires

1. **Tan Tien Fire (Abdomen):** Feel the energy behind the navel become warm as you direct a golden sunshine smile down from your face. Imagine that your energy in the abdomen is like a fireball behind the navel, and below, a stove burning with fire. The stove is situated below the navel and close to the sacrum and lumbar vertebrae. Create the fireball above the stove behind the navel. The Taoists describe it as a burning stove that energizes the other fires in the body.

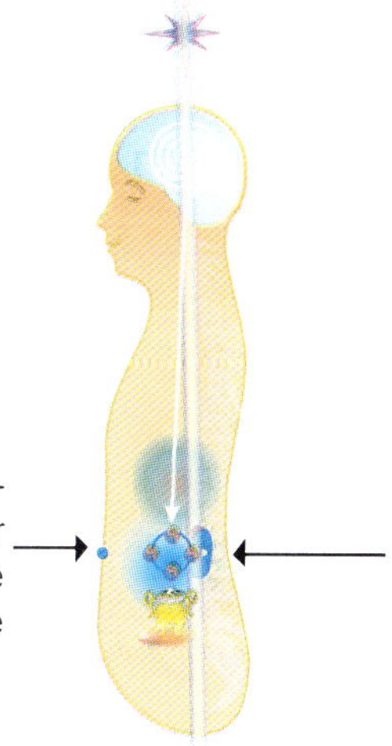

Smile down to the abdomen to create a burning stove near the lower lumbar and sacrum. Create a fire ball behind the navel above the stove.

2. **Fire under the Sea (Kidney):** Be aware of the yang energy of the Adrenals atop the Kidneys. Move that yang energy down into the center of each kidney at the Door of Life (Yang within the Yin), thus lighting the Fire under the Sea. Expand the activated kidneys' energy to the Door of Life point on the spine opposite the navel just below the kidneys.

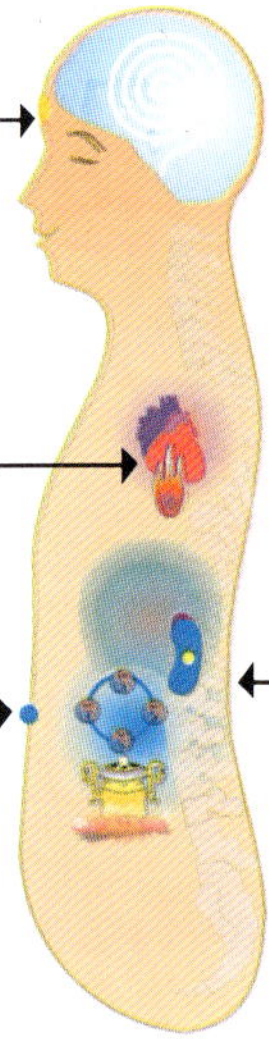

3. **Imperial Fire (Heart):** Activate the consciousness by smiling down to the Heart making it feel soft. Be aware of the Fire in the Heart. Feel the fire of love, joy, happiness, and compassion creating softness in the Heart (Yin within the Yang). This will activate the consciousness of the Heart. Make a triangle, connecting the heart down to the kidneys and then down to the fireball behind the navel (Tan Tien). Connect the fireball to the kidneys and back to the Heart. This triangulation doubles or triples the Chi Fire Power.

Fuse the three minds into one mind *(Yi)*: When the abdomen is filled with Chi and feels warm and nice, it will rise and fill the upper brain with Chi. Lower the upper mind to the lower Tan Tien and the middle mind to the lower Tan Tien, combining the three minds into one mind, ***Yi***. The three mind powers will move to the mideye. You can use this ***Yi*** to make correct decisions and to take the correct action or non-action.

Expand to the 6 Directions: Combine the power of the three minds with the power of the one mind, ***Yi***. Bring the ***Yi*** power into the third eye and expand it to the Six Directions of the Universe.

Link Personal Stars, Energy Body, and Universe: With the ***Yi*** power connect to your ***Personal Star*** six inches above your head. Expand your awareness and consciousness to your personal star and out to the whole universe. If in a group, spiral out and link with their Personal Stars. Create an Energy Body, linking everyone together with the Universe.

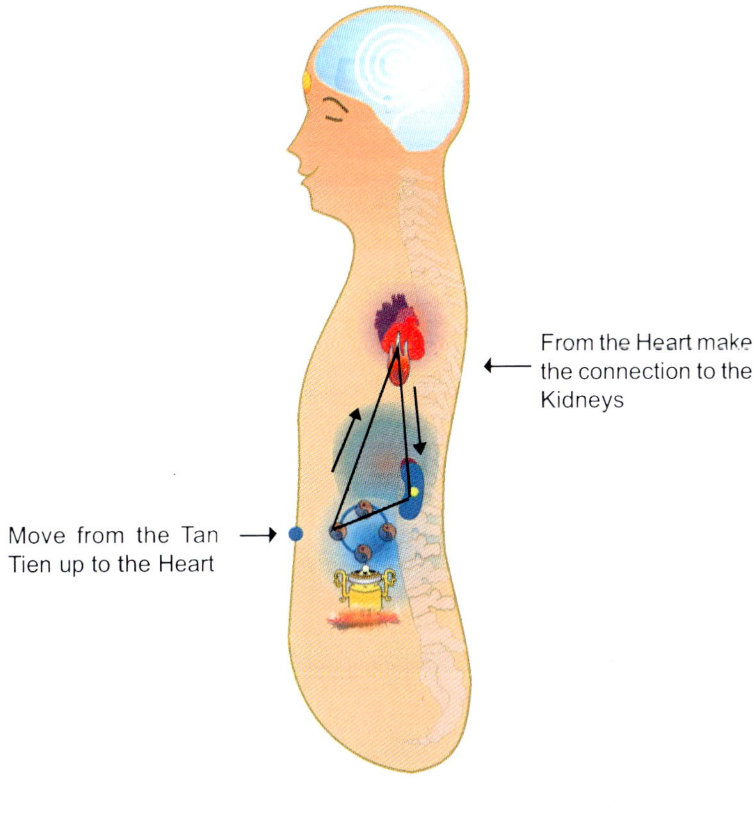

The Triple Force is the Holy Fire:
Make a triangle, Heart to Kidneys to Navel (Tan Tien)

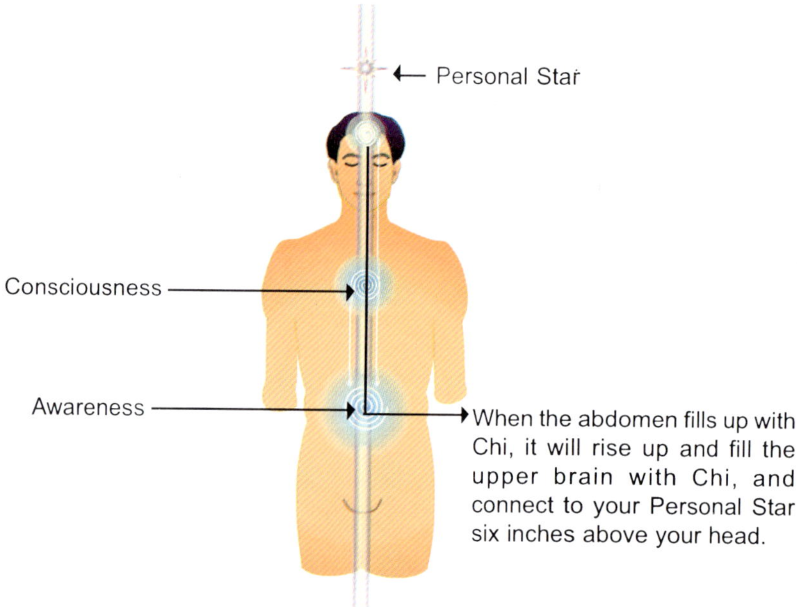

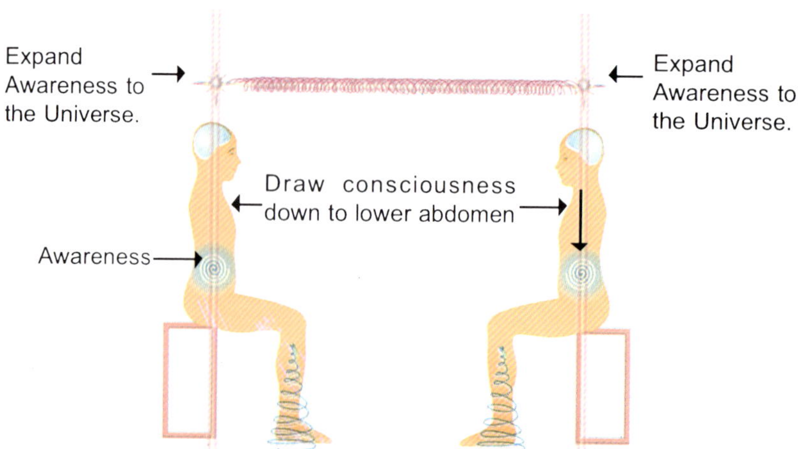

Link with other Personal Stars and expand the awareness from the abdomen.

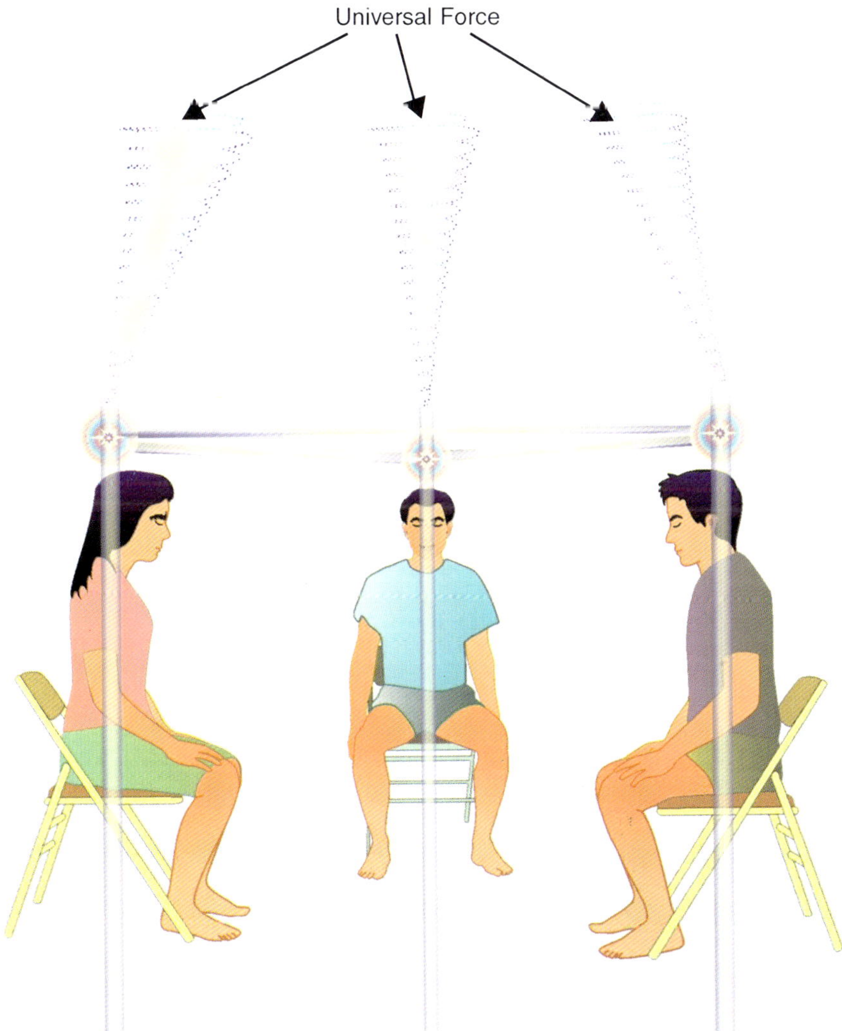

Link with other Personal Stars.

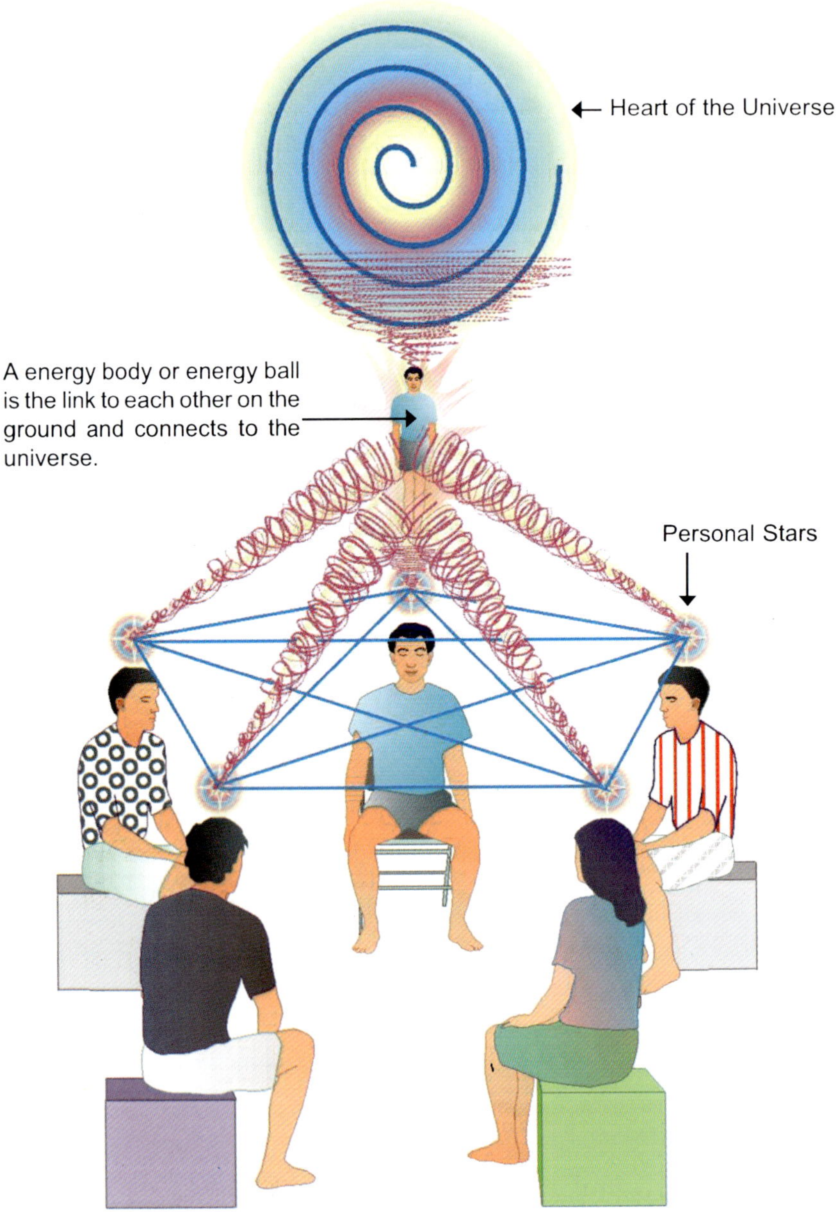

A group can link their Personal Stars together.

Link to friends, instructors, or others in the Healing Tao, or others who are doing similar work.

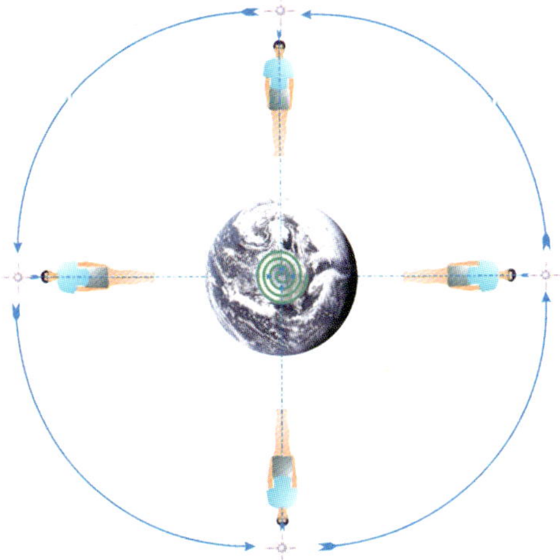

Like a satellite, the World Link meditators become a communication link between the earth and the universe.

Linking to the Heart of the Universe (God) is being in Unconditional Love.

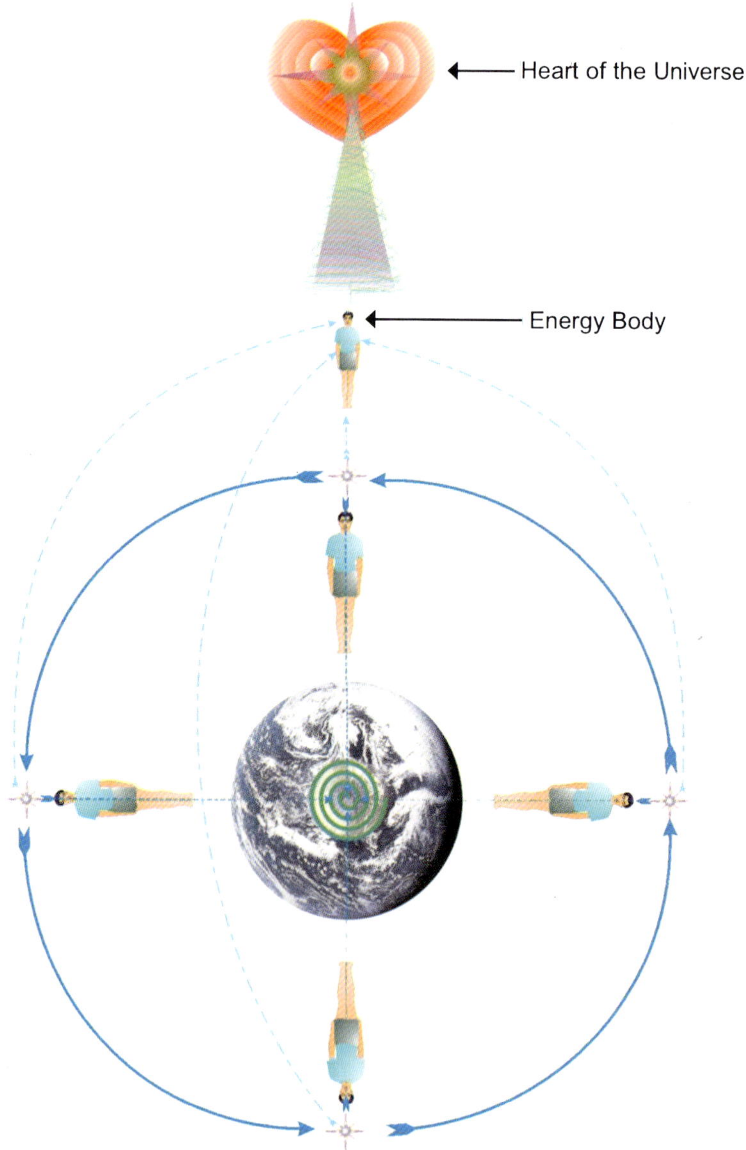

The *Energy Command Communication Center* for each person and group can connect to their own Heart of the Universe.

Protective Sacred Circle of Fire:

The ***Sacred Circle of Fire*** has the power to protect us from all evil, whether it be sickness, misfortune, or negative thinking from those around us. It allows us to connect with the power of the universe. It helps us remove doubts of our own worthiness, so that we may reclaim the best that life has to offer — our birthright. Additionally, the ***Protective Ring*** connects us with the elemental essences of Forces in the Universe which both strengthen and protect us.

Sacred Fire Circle and Golden Chi Field:

This method is entirely an inner visualization using the power of the three minds (the observation, consciousness, and awareness) fused into one mind, the **Yi**. Its purpose is to get in touch with the ***Guardian Essence (aka Guardian Angel)*** or the forces of the ***Six Protective Guardian Animals*** of the ***Six Directions.***

The *Sacred Fire Circle* and *Golden Chi Field* have the power to protect us from evil and negative thinking from around us.

Visualization into Actualization:

When we use the awareness and consciousness, we turn our visualization into actualization using our trust and believe we can manifest it and let it happen in consciousness and awareness with good intentions.

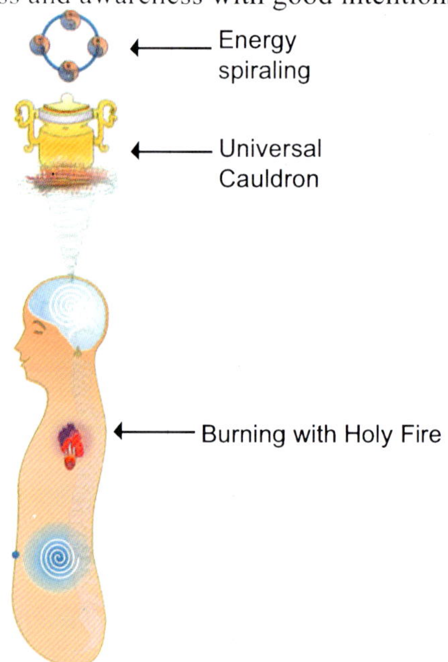

Project a cauldron of fire burning in the Cosmos.

1. Use visualization and imagine a big cauldron burning with fire in the cosmos. Feel the awareness and let it happen.

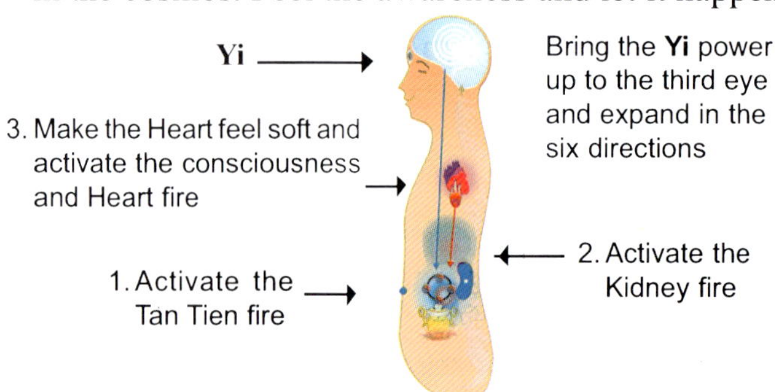

2. Be aware of yourself holding a long wand. Reach out to the cauldron and **ignite the wand** with fire.

3. Use the **Yi** power to draw on the ground with the burning wand a Circle of Fire 7 feet (2 meters) in diameter.

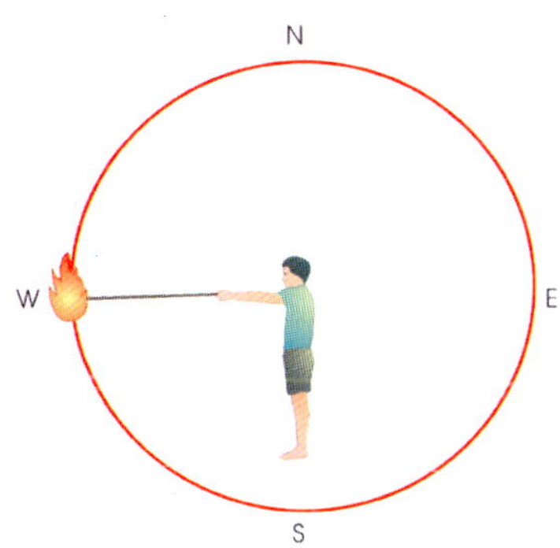

4. Stand in the center. Face the North. Imagine the burning wand and light up the Northern section outside the circle with fire. Pass the wand in an arc towards the South edge of the circle and ignite the Southern section with fire. Then swing it to the Eastern edge and ignite that section with fire.

Light up the North

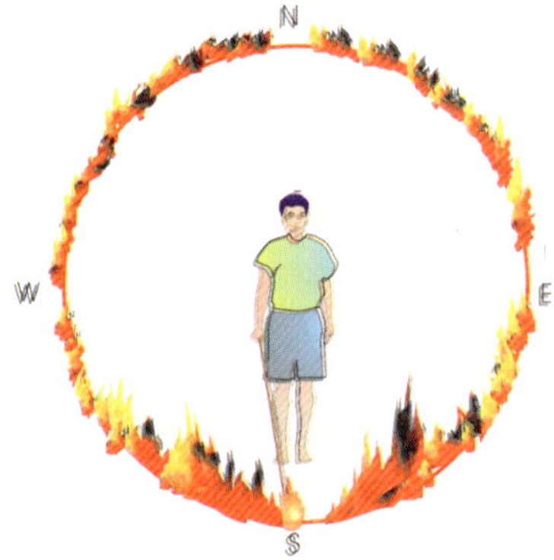

Light up the South

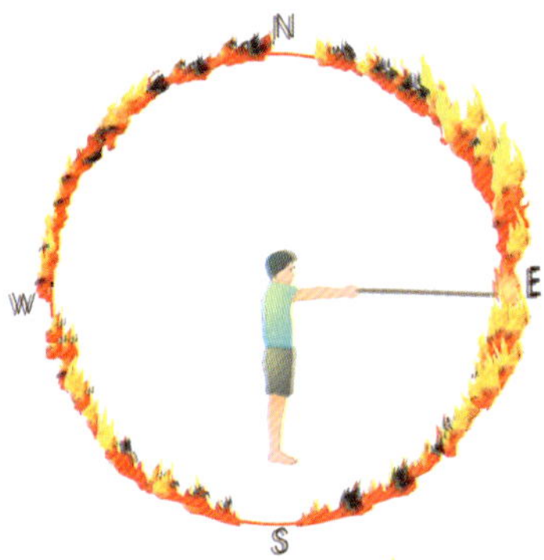

Light up the East

Light up the West

5. Position the wand directly overhead. Turn left to face West and ignite it with fire.
6. Expand the fire to the whole circle, protecting you from all evil, whether it be in the form off sickness, misfortune, or negative thinking from those around you. Place the wand at the edge of the circle.
7. Squat down facing North. In each direction place a Protective Animal (Guardian Essence or Angel): In front (North) place a Blue Tortoise, in back (South) a Red Pheasant, Right (East) a Green Dragon, Left (West) a White Tiger, Above (Center) a Yellow Phoenix, and Below (Earth) a Black Tortoise.

8. Create a protective ***Golden Dome Chi Field*** over you. Let go of all concerns and empty yourself. Ask each animal for protection. These Protective Animals of the 6 Directions are the same protective animals that are associated with the vital organs. Therefore, for energetic protection, ask the Blue Tortoise for Gentleness; Red Pheasant for Joy; Green Dragon for *Kindness*; White Tiger for *Courage*; Yellow Phoenix for *Fairness*; and Black Tortoise for Stillness (Beneath). Connect with Universal Love, saying ***"I am worthy of Divine Love and Protection"***.
9. Remain in this position for several minutes. Be aware of the Sacred Fire burning all around the circle and the ***Golden Dome Chi Field*** surrounding you. This forms a permanent magnetic Sacred Circle that is literally indestructible.

Practice:

Part 1: Affirmations:

Peace within your own Heart

Calm the mind, emptying down to the abdomen and expand the awareness out to the Universe, repeating the following affirmations from the center of your awareness and the consciousness.

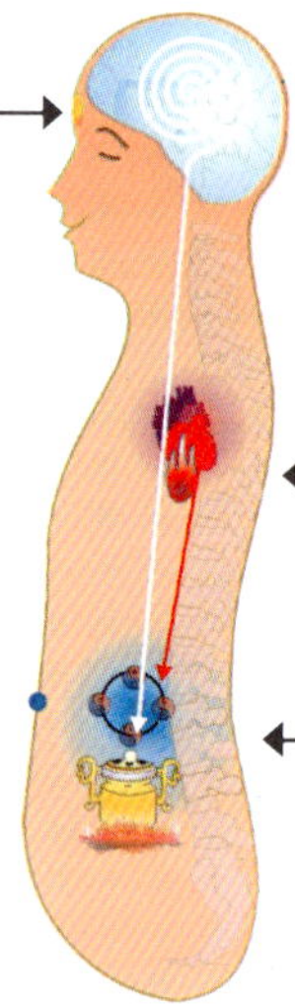

Empty the mind by smiling to the lower Tan Tien and direct the conscious mind of the heart down to the awareness of the lower Tan Tien, combining the three minds to fuse into the one mind ***(Yi)***. The ***(Yi)*** mind is the most powerful mind to connect with the Universe.

I am at peace feeling love & compassion in Myself (Touch Heart).
I am calm,warm, and still in my Center (Touch Lower Abdomen).
I am at peace with my Family and people close to me (Picture Them).
I am at peace with my Neighbors (Picture Them).
I am at peace with my Friends and Co-workers (Picture Them).
I am at peace with my Community (Picture Them).

Part 2: Healing Yourself and Others: *Personal Connection*

1) Empty the Mind by starting a smile in your face. Let the Smiling Energy flow down to the neck and in to the Heart area (the seat of consciousness). Make the heart feel soft and full of love, joy and happiness activating the Conscious mind.
2) Continue smiling and relaxing down to the abdomen (the center of awareness). Smile emptying the mind and senses (eyes, ears, nose and mouth) down until the navel area feels warm activating the Awareness.
3) Feel the Observing Mind of the head and the Conscious Mind of the Heart going down to combine with the Awareness Mind of the Lower Tan Tien. Combine and fuse these three minds into one mind: ***"Yi"*** (pronounced "ee") at the mideye. Expand the awareness out from the abdomen beyond your physical limits to the Cosmos and Universe, connecting with the Universal Energy (God).

Take the **Yi** and spiral it upwards through the crown into the vast pool of energy in the Universe. Continue spiraling in the Universe and let it multiply. Then, spiral it down to your Personal Star and into your whole body.

A. ***Forest Green Energy:*** Picture an ancient forest with bright green leaves up in the Universe. Picture a beautiful emerald green light coming from Heaven and spiral it down to you. Spiral the green light down through your community, Tao Garden, your house, and then into your crown. Let it clean your whole body — binding and absorbing any negativity, burdens, worries, and sick energy, and draining it all out of your body. Let it flow down deep into the ground. Dig a hole and bury the sick negative energy in the ground. Let your heart be happy (3-6 times), for serious illness (36-81 times).

Forest Green Energy: Keep the Tan Tien warm and expand the **Yi** mind to the universe picturing a beautiful emerald green light in the universe.

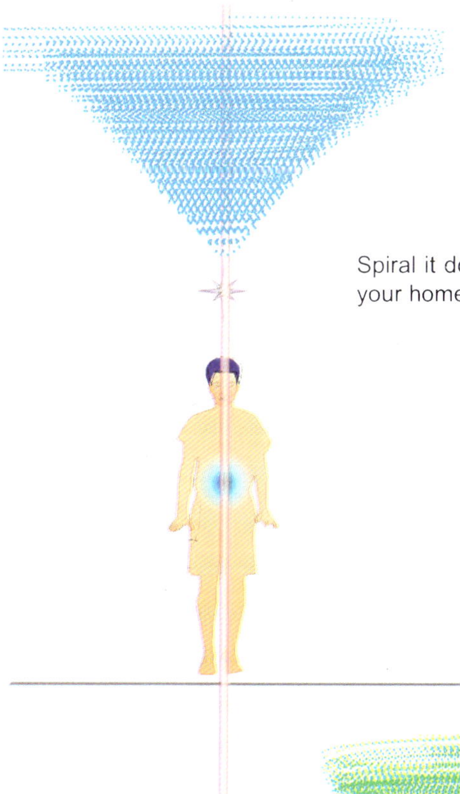

Spiral it down - through your community,
your home, and then into your crown.

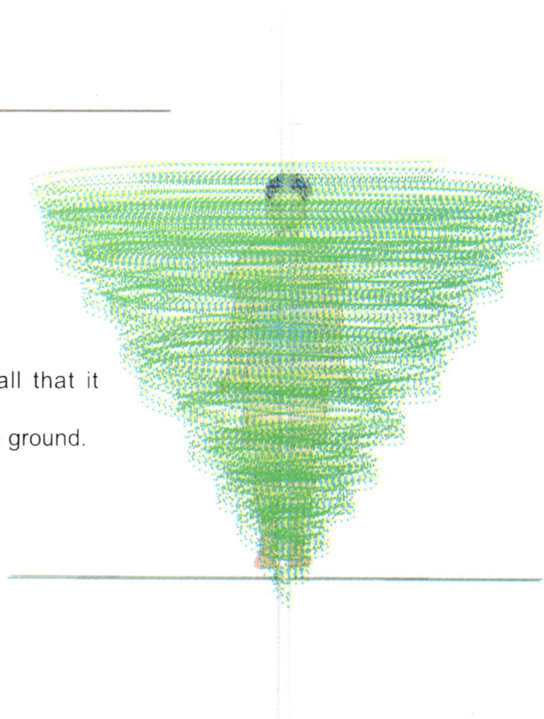

Let the energy cleanse all that it comes in contact with.
Then spiral it down into the ground.

B. ***Ocean/Sky Blue Energy:*** Picture an Ocean/Sky Blue light cooling down your body rinsing and flushing it out like water. Let a blue Light spiral down, increasing in power, spiraling down through your community and your home, then into your crown and into your whole body. Let it flush out all the remaining sickness, negativity and residues down into the ground (3 times).

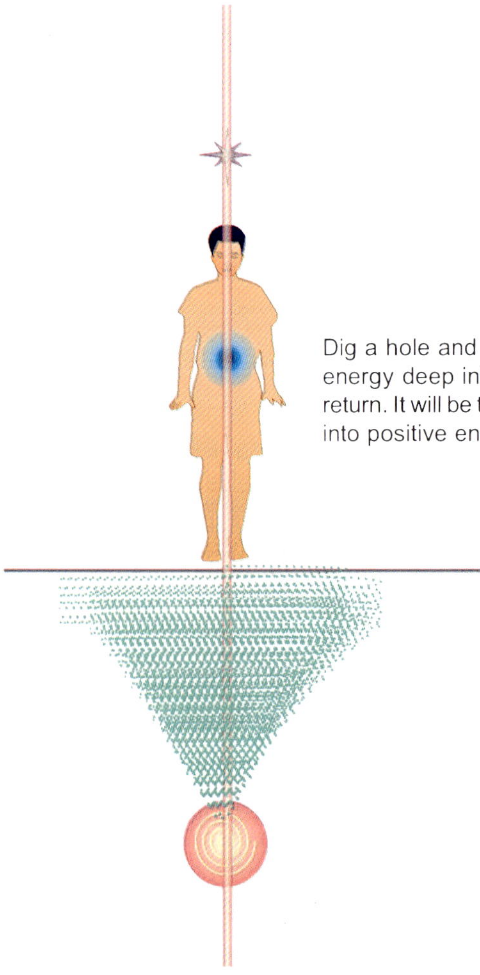

Dig a hole and bury the sick, negative energy deep into the ground, never to return. It will be transformed by the earth into positive energy.

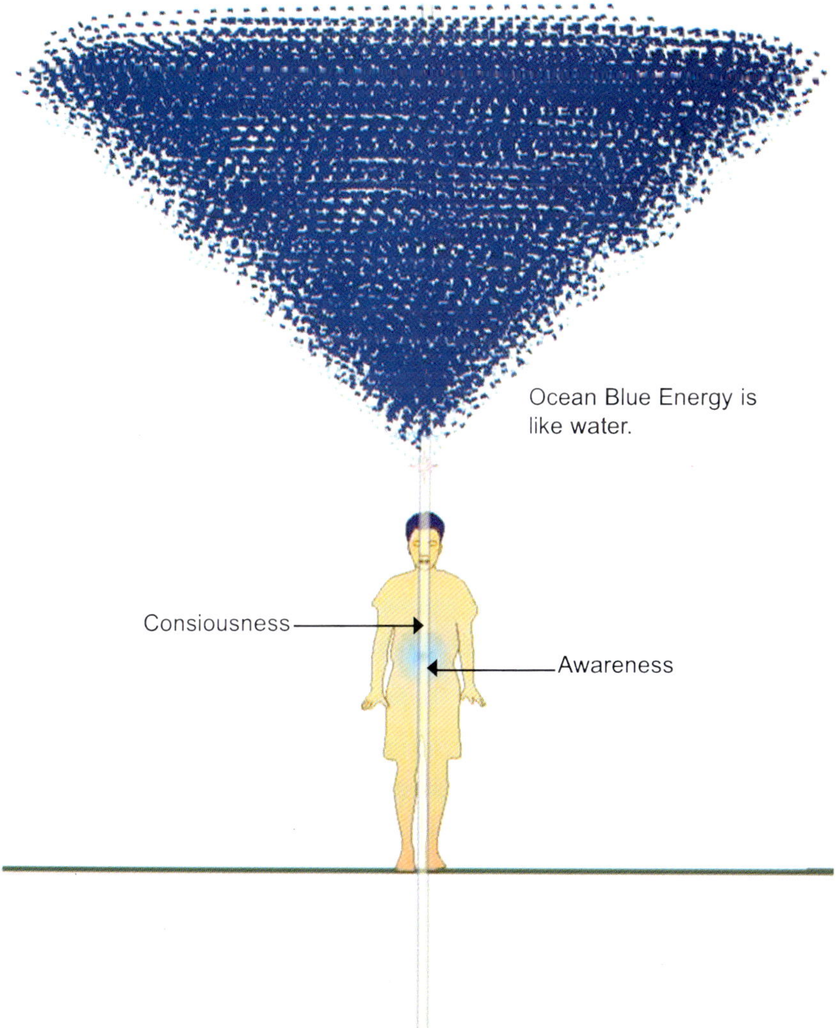

Keep the Tan Tien warm.
Stay connected to the awareness and consciousness of the Yi as you flush the blue light through your body.

C. ***Electric/Universal Violet Energy:*** Picture violet light, the most abundant energy in the Universe. Picture it coming from the North Star and the Big Dipper. Gather the energy in the cup of the Big Dipper. Hold the handle and pour the violet down over the Crown. Spiral the energy down and fill all the cells of your body, together with the Energy Body (6 times).

The North Star is a major source of violet light.
The Big Dipper is a major source of red and infra-red light.

D. *Healing and Strengthening the Whole Body:*

1. Fill the Brain with violet light, saying "Let all sickness go away and let the brain be at its very best."
2. Follow that method for your organs. Using the same affirmation for every organ. You can group the organs with the affirmations:

   a) Eyes, ears, nose, mouth, tongue, teeth.

   b) Thyroid, parathyroid, thymus, pancreas, prostate.

   c) Lungs, heart, stomach, small intestines, large intestines.

   d) Liver, spleen, kidneys, uterus, ovaries, testicles.

Doing this with your mind, stay conscious of the Lower Tan Tien. Expand your awareness to the Universe and the Universe will fill you with healing energy.

E. *Activate the Immune System and Defense System:*

1. Touch the sacrum and feel your fingers grow long with Chi and penetrate into the sacrum and bone marrow,

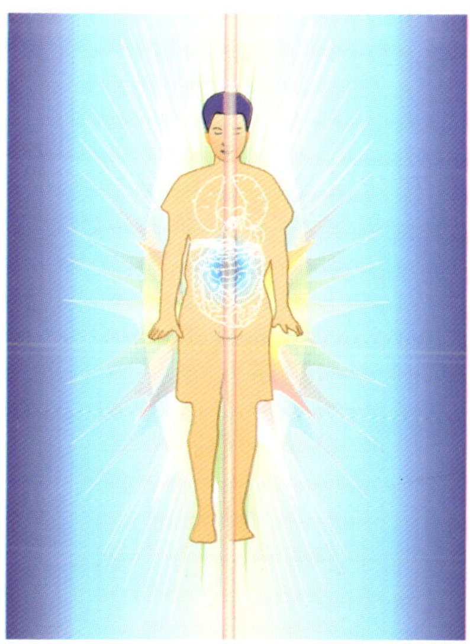

Feel your whole body radiate, clean and shining with light.

activating the bone marrow. Put your mind into the Tan Tien and the Universe. Hold until the Universe fills the sacrum and rises up the spine to the forehead. Feel the pulsating in the temple bones. This increases the production of healthy white blood cells for the immune system. Keep the Tan Tien warm and feel the Chi flow up the spinal cord, then let it spiral up into the Universe. The universe will fill you with healing energy.

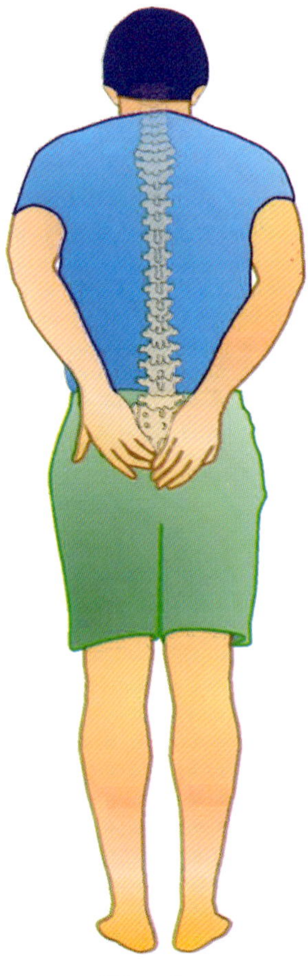

Hold until the Universe fills the sacrum and rises up the spine to the forehead

Activate the Immune System. Empty the mind down. Keep the Tan Tien warm. Touch above the pubic bone and feel your fingers grow long with Chi. Let them penetrate into the sacrum and bone marrow to activate the immune system's production of red and white blood cells. Leave your fingers there and lower your mind into the Tan Tien and the Universe. Feel the funny, happy, laughing, and tingling electrifying sensations in the bones.

Touch and feel the bone. Leave your fingers there. Lower your mind into the Tan Tien and the Universe

Touch the sternum and letting the Chi spread through the sternum through the whole rib cage in the Tan Tien and the Universe, activating production of white blood cells.

Touch the femur bone's middle point (upper legs) and feel your fingers grow long, penetrating the bone marrow of your legs. This should give a tingling sensation through the whole leg. It also increases the production of red blood cells.

Touch the middle part of the femur bone, to help increase the production of healthy red blood cells.

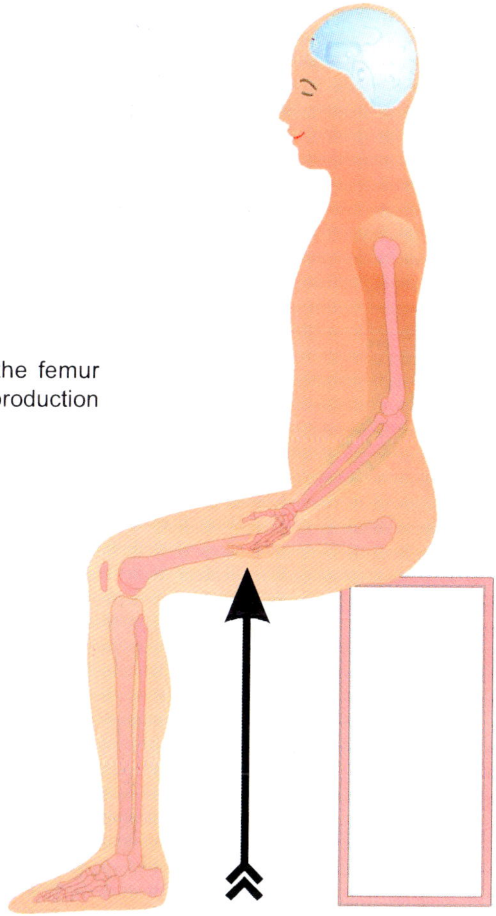

Touch the middle point of femur bones.

1. Touch the middle point of the humerus (upper arm) and feel your fingers grow long permeating the bone marrow of the arm activating production of healthy red blood cells.

Touch the Humerus

2. Touch the sternum, feeling your fingers grow long and project the Chi into the chest cavity activating the thymus gland. Feel the connection to the thyroid and parathyroid glands. This activates the immune system and increases the production of the T-cells (the anti-virus commando cells of the body).

Touch the Sternum

Part 3: Manifestations:
Virtue Mind Power
Our Subconscious Guilt

In order to increase the Virtue Mind Power, you need to get rid of subconscious guilt. Our subconscious guilt-complexes are major obstacles to our health and progress. They are the major causes of illness and frustrations. It is as if we have an inner program that says we do not deserve to have health, wealth and happiness. This guilt makes us feel like powerless victims.

Other guilt-complexes assume that we are sinners requiring punishment in the form of ill health or misfortune. We can never bring ourselves to ask the universe for anything that we do not feel worthy to receive. God made the human in his own image. Humankind is naturally entitled to everything that the earth and the universe can provide for our happiness and well being. As children of God we deserve the best. We can command the Cosmos, providing that we make our command in the right way and with good intent.

Being Unwanted

Being unwanted is one of the worst situations for many people. This is true for all those who feel alone, even children, but especially for old people who might feel left all alone to die. Subconsciously, they will send out messages to the Cosmos to make yourselves sick. However the more attention that is given to sickness and ill health, the more energy is received from the Cosmos to make that happen. We get exactly what is projected by the subconscious mind.

Negative Self-Talk And Negative Thinking

Every thought whether positive or negative is a command to the universe. If our lives are not how we would like them to be, it is because we have unwittingly given negative commands to the Cosmos, thereby getting those results. Humans have a deep need for love and attention. Sometimes we become needy and try to get sympathy and attention through being sick, or by becoming a victim. If in our subconscious we believe that our motives are unrighteous or impure, then the Cosmos will keep us poor, sick, or both.

Your command to the Cosmos always brings results. We get exactly what we command, whether good or bad. Therefore, we must be careful of what we think, feel and say, if we want our lives changed for the better. We can remove all the unworthy, guilty, sinful thoughts and philosophy, replacing them with the realization that we are the Children of God (the Cosmos). We can accept the best the Universe and Earth have to offer. Be glad to see other people have honestly-gained wealth, health and happiness. If we develop jealous or negative feelings towards them, then we immediately return to the state of being self-righteously poor.

We need not accept the results of our negative thinking. We can initiate a positive course of action. To fully use this power you must replace negative thought patterns with our new command of the cosmic force. You must take action when you receive the energy and information. The way to get extra energy is by breathing the red light into the heart 3 to 6 times letting it radiate into the whole body into the heart. You will feel alot of energy helping you to take the actions necessary to complete your tasks.

Direct Command

To make a positive statement is to make a direct command. A command given in the present tense – in the now – is the most powerful command to the Cosmos that we can give. A command to the Cosmos should be phrased clearly as an individual statement and always be said aloud.

For example, if we make the command to ourselves, ***"I am well, I am healthy, I am happy, I am wealthy,"*** it doesn't matter how sick or poor we are. The fact is, we have already begun to take on that quality because of the command that we have given. The change will begin very rapidly. The Cosmic force will begin work on our inner functions immediately, according to what qualities we have claimed. Success in using Cosmic power depends upon our working with, and our exercise of, the command in the right way to take action and responsibility. Practicing Positive Mind Power, fusing the three minds into one, the Inner Smile, or Chi Kung will help.

Once you have set the cosmic force in motion with a direct command, you must take action. You must be willing to take responsibility for yourself. The universe can not accomplish everything on its own. The key is to use the Cosmic force to aid your actions. There is no limit to what the individual can accomplish when combining the Cosmic force with individual intent.

Manifestations: Yi Mind Power

Start with smiling, and empty the mind to fuse the three minds as one (**Yi**) in the lower abdomen. Move the Chi up to open the frontal lobe of the brain at the Third Eye. Create a triangle from the third eye to the temple bones filling it with Chi. Expand the awareness to the universe.

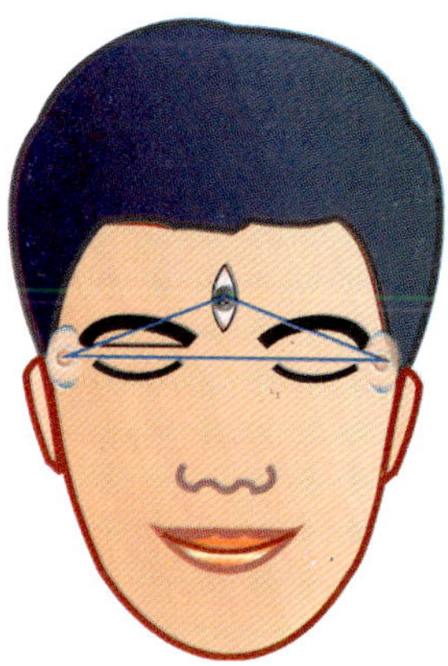

Third eye and temple bones are in a Triangle

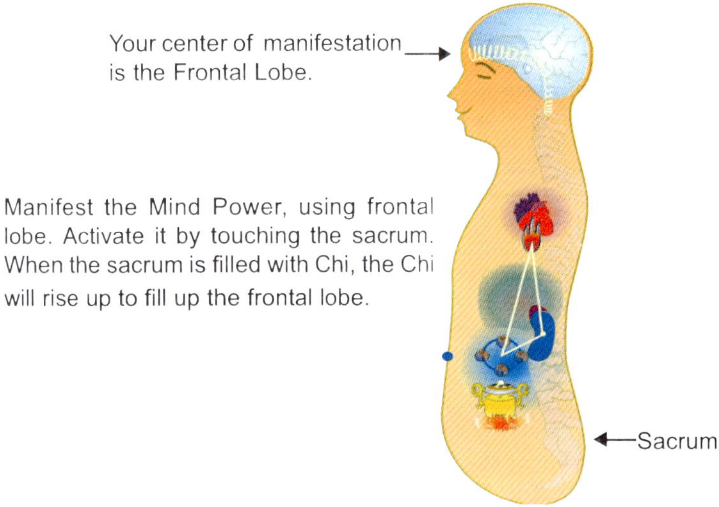

We manifest our affirmations in the physical, emotional, mental, and spritual body by starting to manifest from the center of your awareness by placing your attention in the abdomen. Next bring the thought that you want to manifest up to the heart connection, then to the upper mind, the frontal lobe, and the middle eye brow. Broadcast it out to the whole Universe. This affirmation is multiplied many times over by the abundant energy of the Universe. It will return to you to be manifested, but you must wait with your awareness anchored in the second brain - the lower abdomen.

A. ***Physical Image:*** Picture yourself at an age you would like to be, anu hold that image very clearly. Hold it in the center of your second brain (lower abdomen) and move it up to the center of your consciousness, in the heart area. Continue to hold this image very clearly and move it up to the forehead and then send it out to the Universe in all six directions, saying, ***"I am well and perfectly healthy."***

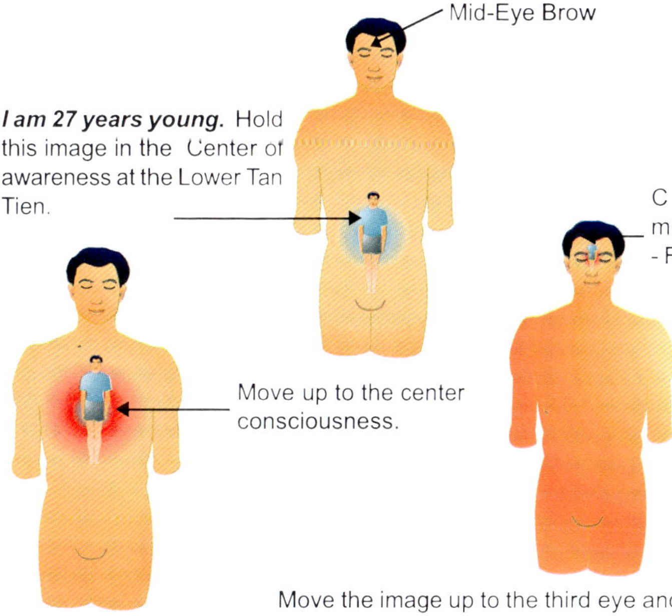

I am 27 years young. Hold this image in the Center of awareness at the Lower Tan Tien.

Move up to the center consciousness.

Move the image up to the third eye and intensify it.

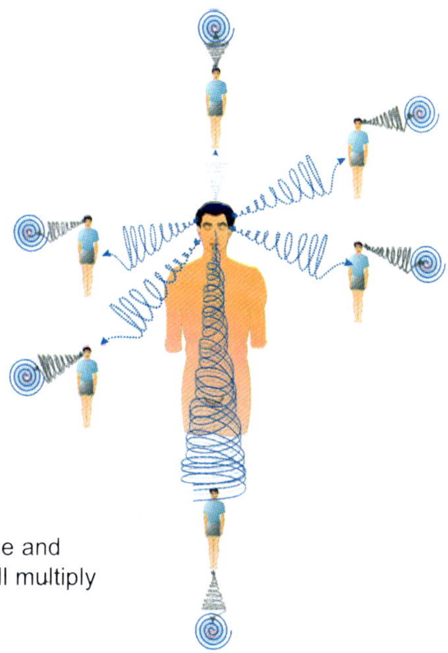

Send the image out into the Universe and all six directions. The affirmation will multiply and return to you to be manifested.

B. ***Emotional Image:*** Picture your emotional body: See a body-shaped image close around your physical body, composed of all kinds of moving colors, saying: ***"I let go of old emotional experiences, seeing them for what they are, and fill myself with radiant joy, love, and compassion."*** Bring the image up the heart center and then to the frontal lobe. Send it out to the Universe and the Universe will multiply it many times and it will be sent back to you. Just wait for it to return with your awareness in the lower brain.

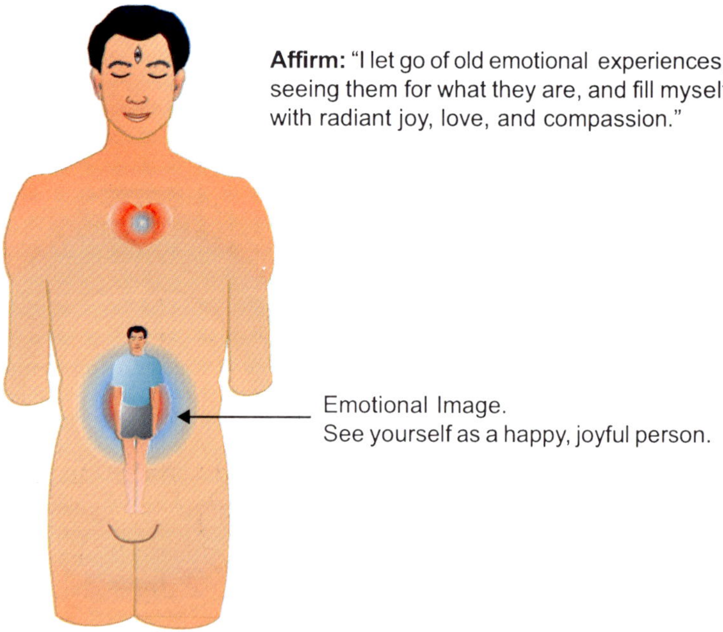

C. ***Mental Image:*** Picture your mental body, saying: ***"I make an agreement with myself to enjoy the best of life and to live to my full wealth potential in harmony with Nature and the Universe."*** Follow the same sequence of moving the image up to the heart, the frontal lobe, and out to the Universe. Wait for the return with your awareness in the lower brain.

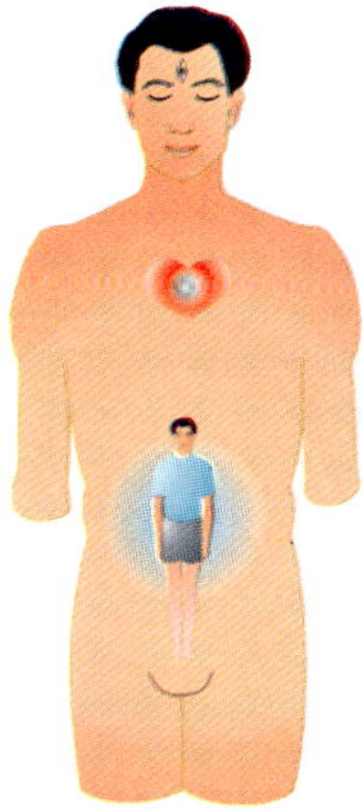

Affirm: "I make an agreement with myself to enjoy the best of life and to live to my full wealth potential."

D. ***Spiritual Image:*** Picture your spiritual body and higher self, saying: ***"I am at one with my God (Source) within and manifest its Glory."*** Follow the same procedure as before.

Part 4: Problem Solving: *Answers and Solutions*

A. Take the questions and problems that you have into your center of ***Awareness*** (Abdominal Brain) then to your ***Consciousness*** (Heart Brain) and send them out into the universe through the third eye in your ***Observation*** center (Mind Brain) broadcasting out to the Whole Universe.

B. Wait for the best answers and solutions to return to you clearly and distinctly. Allow them to ripen into full understanding.

C. At any point in the future, if you have any questions or you need to take action or a problem to be solved, all you need to do is to inhale deeply and allow your awareness in the abdomen to expand far beyond your physical limits.

D. Exhale your problem into the Universe, open yourself, wait for a moment and let go of the problem. You will become conscious of the solutions to your questions or problems you presented. The more you practice this, the quicker and easier the results will come. You must take action when you receive the energy and information. The way to get extra energy is by breathing red light into the heart 3 to 6 times, letting it radiate into the whole body through the heart. You will feel alot of energy enabling you to take action and complete the task.

E. You can use the same technique to project the goals and the time-frame during which you wish to accomplish them. Sometimes it helps to ask for more wisdom from the Universe or Cosmos in order to understand our Life's purpose.

Finish the meditation by resting for a few moments and collecting the energy in your Lower Tan Tien.

Conclusion:

The purpose of this meditation is to be:

Happy with ourselves in order to heal ourselves.
Happy to help and heal others.
Happy to create, project, and manifest our goals, and to accomplish them in a virtuous way.

We wish you the very best that life has to offer.

Yours in the Tao,
Mantak Chia

International Healing Tao
Tao Garden Training Center
274/1 Moo 7, Luang Nua, Doi Saket,
Chiang Mai 50220, Thailand.
Tel: (66)(53) 865-034 Fax: (66)(53) 495-852
Email: taogarden@hotmail.com & healingt@loxinfo.co.th
Website: www.internationalhealingtao.com